MIKE YOU…

SUPERTED AND THE INCA TREASURE

Illustrations by Tony Hutchings

Muller

SuperTed and his pal Spottyman were talking to a worried museum curator who pointed to a very old map as he spoke. 'Somewhere deep in the heart of this South American jungle, where no man has set foot for almost a thousand years, lies a forgotten temple of an ancient civilisation . . . the Incas. The Incas hid their treasures in this temple. Plenty of gold and jewels.'

'And you want these treasures for your museum?' asked SuperTed.

'Yes, that is so, here they will be safe from thieves.'

Spottyman said, 'Don't worry Mr. Rodriguez, whenever there's trouble we're always first on the spot.'

Meanwhile deep in the jungle, Skeleton dragged a heavy canoe up a muddy riverbank.

'It's not fair, why do I always get the rotten jobs?' grumbled Skeleton.

Texas Pete studied a map and said, 'According to this map, the Inca temple should be a short pony ride through those trees.'

Bulk, munched some Brazil nuts, shells and all, and said, 'But we haven't got a short pony, Tex.'

'That's never stopped us before . . . now come on, let's get moving,' shouted Tex.

Despite the terrific heat, Skeleton shivered and complained. 'Why do we have to come through this terrible jungle? Ugh! It's crawling with beetles and snakes! It's revolting.'

'Yeah,' replied Bulk. 'It's revolting, terrible, disgusting . . . but I like it.' And off they trudged.

At that moment SuperTed and Spottyman came flying through the sky above them in Spotty's rocketship.

In his funny Spotty voice he said, 'This looks like the right jungle, SuperTed.'

'Yes, but where's the temple, Spotty?'

Down in the jungle, Skeleton noticed the spacecraft and shouted, 'What's that in the sky, Tex?'

Texas Pete recognised it immediately. 'It's that Spotty sausage that Spottyman flies, stand clear fellas, give me room.' He drew his guns and fired into the air and hit the rocketship.

'Pulsating Prunes!' cried SuperTed. 'We've been hit! Bale out Spotty.'

Spottyman jumps out of the craft, realising too late that he's forgotten both his parachute and rocket pack. 'Help meeee . . .'

SuperTed whispers his very secret word which only he knows. Whoosh, he changes from an ordinary teddy into the brave Superbear and flies out of the damaged spacecraft, his booster rockets on his boots at full power. He catches Spotty. 'Got you! . . . Phew . . . Just in time.'

Spotty is very grateful. 'You may be furry SuperTed, but you're no kitten.'

'Come on Spotty, let's find that temple.'

But someone has beaten them to it. Bulk, Skeleton and Texas Pete climb up the temple steps. They are panting, the heat is terrific. A gorilla grunts as it watches them from the jungle.

Texas shouts at Skeleton, 'Hurry up lazy bones.'

'Bones? Don't be personal,' replies Skeleton crossly.

Tex orders Bulk to break down the temple door. Fat Bulk tries and hurts his shoulder.

Bulk and Tex each climb on to a stone gorilla's lap. Skeleton scrambles on to the third gorilla's lap. Third gorilla?

'Help, it's real,' he screamed. The jungle gorilla has pretended to be a statue.

Bulk thought it was funny too, and he accidentally hit the stone gorilla's arm. This was a secret lever which opened the door of the temple.

Later SuperTed and Spottyman arrive at the temple to find it already open.

'Looks as if we're too late Spotty.'

They peer inside and Spotty says, 'Maybe they're still in there.'

SuperTed is just a little afraid, 'It's dark in there . . . You go first Spotty.'

'No, after you. It takes longer for my Spotty eyesight to adjust.'

'All right,' the brave bear replied. 'Here goes.'

Inside the temple they hear strange echoing sounds. 'Gold! Yahoo we're rich.'

'Bubbling Blancmange! Did you hear that Spotty?'

'Sounded like nothing on Spot,' gulped the frightened Spottyman.

'Spottyman, do you believe in the spirits of the Incas?' asked SuperTed.

'No,' croaked Spotty.

'Neither do I. Come on we must get to the bottom of this mystery,' said the brave bear.

They come to the end of the passage and peeping inside the gold room they see Skeleton trying on jewellery. 'Bulk, do you think I look best in diamonds or rubies?'

Then Skeleton and Bulk see SuperTed flying through the passage towards them. 'Oh no . . . Tex help us,' they squeal.

SuperTed pushes Bulk who tumbles head over heels. 'Just as I thought Bulk and Skeleton,' he mutters, 'but where's Texas Pete? '

'Here I am you tatty Teddy, but you won't get me.' At that instant the baddest baddie in the world fires his guns at the roof of the tunnel and dashes through the open door.

The whole tunnel collapses and traps everyone in the gold room.

SuperTed tries with all his might to move a huge boulder which blocks the doorway, but it is too much even for him.

Spottyman says, 'To think I'll never see the planet Spot again.'

Suddenly the gorilla thumps a panel in the wall of the gold room and a secret passage opens. SuperTed thanks the gorilla and says, 'Let's go everyone. It may be dark, it may be damp, but a bear who isn't brave just isn't a bear.'

Outside in the jungle a figure pushes through the undergrowth. 'Heh. heh. heh. That's the last I'll hear of SuperTed. This time I've really settled his hash.'

Inside the temple, SuperTed and his companions are nearing the end of the trail. A deep underground river crosses their path.

'Well Spotty,' says SuperTed, 'There's only one thing for it. There are times when a teddy just has to get his fur wet.' He dives in followed by the others.

Skeleton though says, 'Oooh, it's freezing. I'm not going in there. I'm not!'

The gorilla nudges him and Skeleton changes his mind.

'It's all right. I'm going in, I'm going in!'

Meanwhile Texas Pete has reached his canoe by the river.

'So long, SuperTed, I can't say it's been pleasant knowing you, but I'm kinda sorry we'll never meet again.'

SuperTed suddenly pops up in the water beside the boat and laughs. 'That's what you think.'

Tex moans, 'Oh no! Not that mangy little teddy!'

SuperTed rocks the boat until Tex feels sea sick.

'It's not fair, I never get away with it. I was doing just fine till you came along.'

Later back at the museum . . .

'Thank you SuperTed. I feel happy now the treasures are here where everyone can see them,' said the curator.

'And those thieves locked up,' laughed Spotty.

'Yes,' said SuperTed, 'That'll teach them not to tinker with the Incas.'

Goodbye SuperTed and Spottyman.